Fossil Ridge Public Library District
386 Kennedy Road
Braidwood, Illinois 60408

1/01

An Online Visit to
AUSTRALIA

Edit View Go Bookmarks Communicator Help

Back Forward Reload Home Search Images Print Security Stop

Netsite:

What's Related

Erin M. Hovanec

The Rosen Publishing Group's
PowerKids Press™
New York

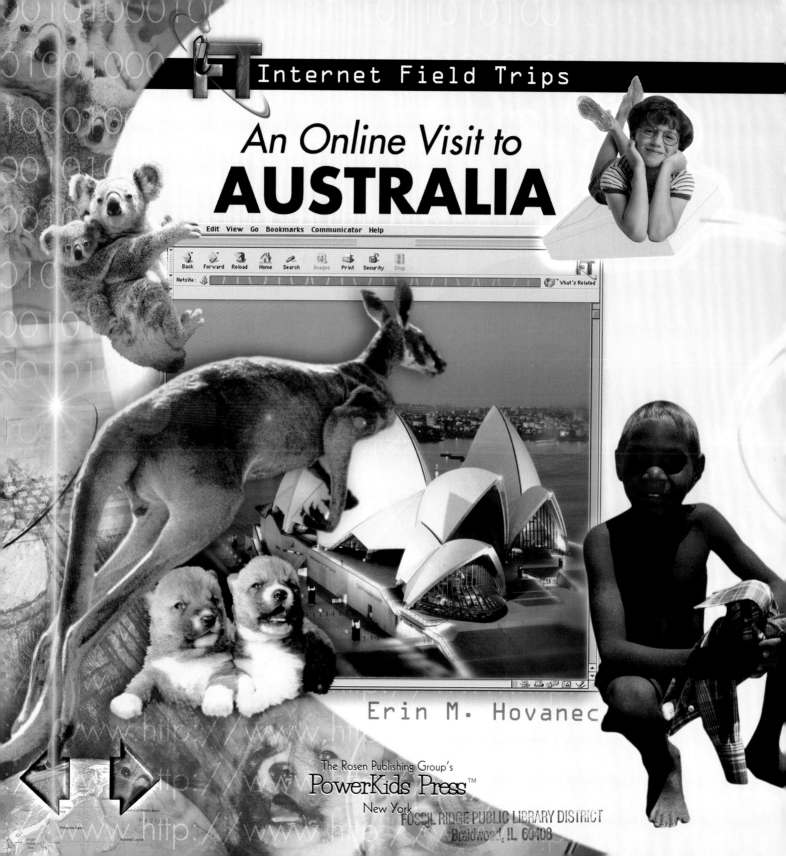

For my dad, Joseph Hovanec

Published in 2001 by The Rosen Publishing Group, Inc.

29 East 21st Street, New York, NY 10010

First Edition

Book Design: Maria Melendez

Photo Credits: Cover, title page, Koala © International Stock; Kangaroo, Dingo Puppies © SuperStock; title page, Sydney Opera House © H. Armstrong Roberts; title page, Aboriginal Boy © Robert Garvey/CORBIS; title page, tortoise drawing © Rallph A. Clevenger/CORBIS; p. 7 © Patrick Ward/CORBIS; p. 8 © Paul A. Souders/CORBIS; p. 19 © Penny Tweedie/CORBIS; p. 20 © Dallas and John Heaton/CORBIS; p. 16 © Reuters Newmedia Inc./CORBIS; p.11 © International Stock; p. 12 © H. Armstrong Roberts.

Hovanec, Erin M.
     An online visit to Australia / Erin Hovanec.— 1st ed.
       p. cm.— (Internet field trips)
     Includes index.
     Summary: An online trip to various Internet web sites reveals a variety of facts about the only country that is also a continent.
     ISBN 0-8239-5653-9 (alk. paper)
     1. Australia—Computer network resources—Juvenile literature. 2. Australia—Computer network resources—Directories—Juvenile literature. 3. Web sites—Directories—Juvenile literature. 4. World Wide Web (Information retrieval system)—Juvenile literature. [1. Australia.] I. Title.

DU92 .H68 2000
025.06'994—dc21   00-023745

Manufactured in the United States of America

Contents

What You'll Need to Get Started

Your home computer can connect you to the Internet. You can also take a trip to your school library or local public library and start "surfing" there. To surf or to do a search on the Net, you'll need the following:

A personal computer

A computer with a monitor (or screen), a mouse, and a keyboard. You'll need all of these.

A modem

A modem, which will connect your computer to a telephone line, and then to other computers around the world.

A telephone connection

A telephone connection, which uses your modem to talk to other computers through a telephone line.

Internet software

An Internet software program, which tells your computer how to use the Internet.

An Internet Service Provider

There's a growing number of Internet Service Providers that allow you to get on the Internet for a small fee every month.

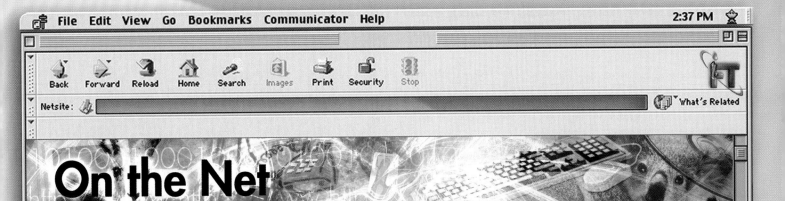

On the Net

How high can kangaroos really jump? What's in the Great Barrier Reef? Want to visit the Outback? You don't need to visit Australia to find out about these things. You can find them all on the Internet! The Internet is basically a bunch of computers connected to each other around the world. You can find just about anything you've ever wanted to know by using a search engine. A search engine is a computer program that sorts through millions of pieces of information. Search for the word "Australia" and the search engine will show you a list of colored words called hyperlinks. Click on a hyperlink with your mouse to find a Web site about Australia.

5

Where's Australia?

Australia is the only country that is also a continent. It's the smallest of the seven continents, but it's the sixth biggest country on Earth. Australia is about three million square miles (7,769,964 sq km). The Indian Ocean lies to the north, west, and south of Australia. The Pacific Ocean is located to the east. Farther north are the countries of Indonesia and Papua New Guinea. The country of New Zealand is about 1,000 miles (1,609 km) southeast of Australia. Australia lies entirely in the Southern Hemisphere. Perhaps that is the reason why Australia is called "the land down under."

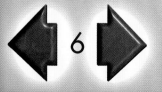

6

Australia is a country and a continent. This photo shows Ayers Rock, a popular Australian landmark. ▶

For more information, and online maps of Australia:
http://www.nationalgeographic.com/expeditions/atlas/ocemenu.html

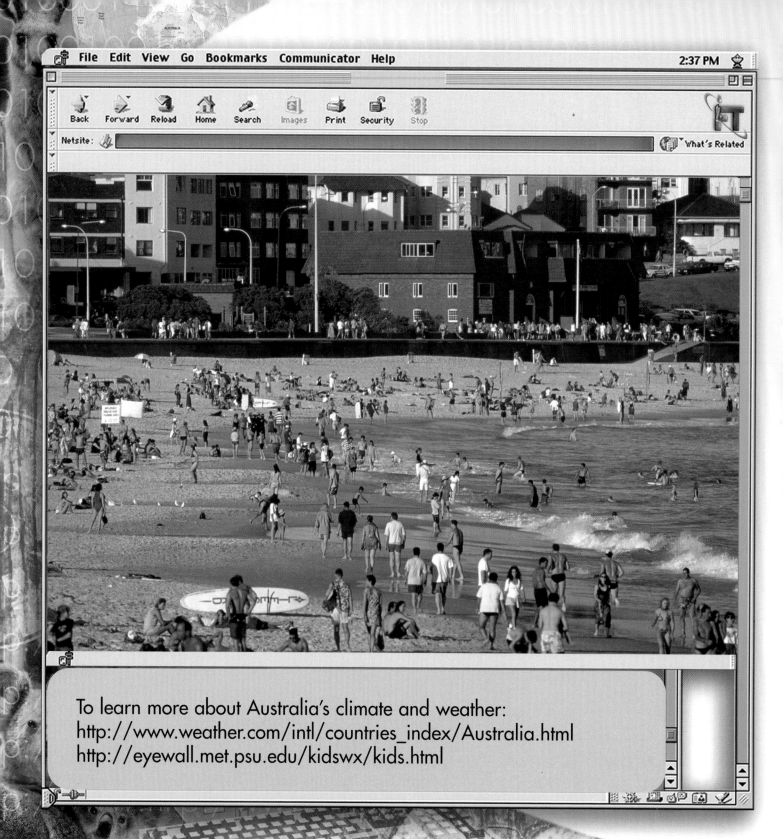

To learn more about Australia's climate and weather:
http://www.weather.com/intl/countries_index/Australia.html
http://eyewall.met.psu.edu/kidswx/kids.html

Summer in December!

The weather in Australia and the Southern Hemisphere can be the exact opposite of the weather in the Northern Hemisphere. The United States, Canada, and Europe are in the Northern Hemisphere. A cold, snowy day in Canada might mean a day at the beach in Australia. Different parts of Australia have different climates. Northern Australia is hot all year long because it is close to the **equator**. The rest of the continent has warm summers and cool winters. About one-third of Australia is hot, dry desert. It rarely snows in most of Australia, but some areas receive lots of rain, as much as 150 inches (381 cm) each year!

◄ *Sunbathers and swimmers enjoy the surf at Bondi Beach in Sydney, Australia.*

9

The Land Down Under

Australia has a **population** of more than 19 million people. That may seem like a lot, but Australia is a very big country! About 85 percent of Australians live in cities. Canberra is the country's capital. Sydney and Melbourne are its largest cities. Australia is made up of six states. The five mainland states are New South Wales, Queensland, South Australia, Victoria, and Western Australia. Tasmania, a state that is also an island, lies off of Australia's southeast coast. Australia also has two mainland territories, the Australia Capital Territory, which contains the city of Canberra, and the Northern Territory.

This is a helicopter view of Sydney, Australia, its harbor, and the Sydney Opera House. ▶

To find out more about Australia's geography:
http://library.thinkquest.org/28994/geo.html
http://www.csu.edu.au/australia

To learn more about the Outback and the Great Barrier Reef:
http://www.pbs.org/edens/kakadu/seasons.html
http://www.ozramp.net.au/~senani/barrier.htm

The Outback and the Reef

Most of Australia is a flat **landmass** called a **plateau**. A popular attraction is Ayers Rock. This huge loaf-shaped rock is in Australia's Western Plateau region. Deserts or dry grasslands called the "Outback" cover large regions of Australia. Remote, hard-to-get-to regions are called "the bush." Deserts cover about one-third of Australia. Australia has several national parks. The Great Barrier Reef in the Pacific Ocean lies off Australia's coast. It is the world's largest **coral reef**. It stretches for more than 1,250 miles (2,012 km). More than 350 types of coral and thousands of different sea creatures live in this reef.

This photo shows the Great Barrier Reef and Green Island off the coast of North Queensland, Australia.

13

Animals Like Nowhere Else

   Australia is home to some of the world's most amazing animals! Many can't be found anywhere else on Earth. There are kangaroos and wallabies, which are smaller kangaroos, koalas, and wild dogs called dingoes. You probably know that kangaroos can jump very high. Some can jump as far as 30 feet (9.1 m). Over 400 species of lizards and 100 species of snakes, including some of the world's deadliest snakes, live in Australia. The saurian crocodile lives there, too. This fierce creature can grow as long as 20 feet (6.1 m). Many unusual birds, like black swans, giant emus that resemble ostriches, and colorful parrots call Australia home.

14

Emus are tall, fast-running birds found in Australia. This emu hen is protecting her eggs.

Back   Forward   Reload   Home   Search   Images   Print   Security   Stop

Netsite: What's Related

To discover more about Australia's animals:
http://www.kipandco.com.au/wildlife_page/wildlife.html
http://www.EnchantedLearning.com/coloring/Australia.shtml

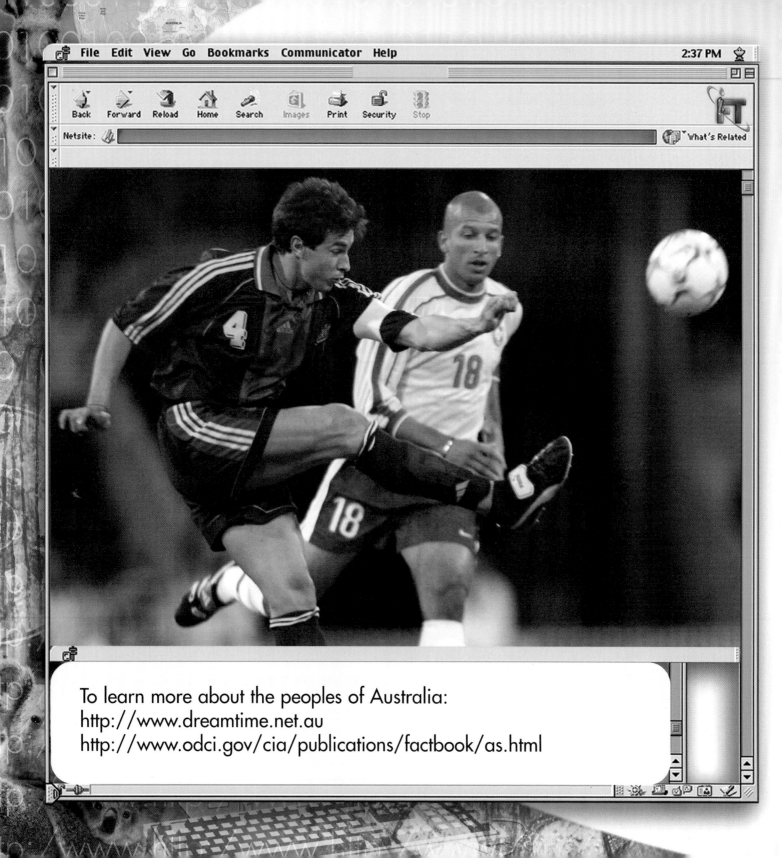

To learn more about the peoples of Australia:
http://www.dreamtime.net.au
http://www.odci.gov/cia/publications/factbook/as.html

What's an "Aussie" Anyway?

People who live in Australia are called Australians or "Aussies." About 96 percent of the country's population is of European **descent**. Most Australians' ancestors came from Great Britain or Ireland during the eighteenth century. People from all over the world now settle in Australia. Native Australian peoples, called **aborigines**, have lived in Australia for tens of thousands of years. They make up a small **ethnic group** that is important to the history of Australia. Until the 1950s, most aborigines lived as **nomads** in the Northern Territory. Today, about 160,000 aborigines live in Australia. Many have adopted modern ways.

◀ *Most Australians enjoy participating in or watching sports. Soccer is the fastest-growing sport in Australia.*

17 ▶

Important Industries

Australians work in many different **industries**. Only about five percent of the country's laborers work in agriculture. However, these people produce enough food to feed everyone in Australia! Many of these farmers raise sheep and cattle. They also grow wheat and sugarcane.

Australian factories manufacture all kinds of goods, including processed foods, clothing, and household items. The mining industry is also very important in Australia. The continent is the world's leading producer of diamonds and lead. It also produces large amounts of many metals, such as copper, gold, iron, nickel, and silver.

Sheep ranching is an important agricultural industry in Australia. This boy lives on a sheep ranch.

To learn more about the Australia's industries:
http://www.atlapedia.com/online/countries/austral.htm
http://www.agso.gov.au/education/factsheet

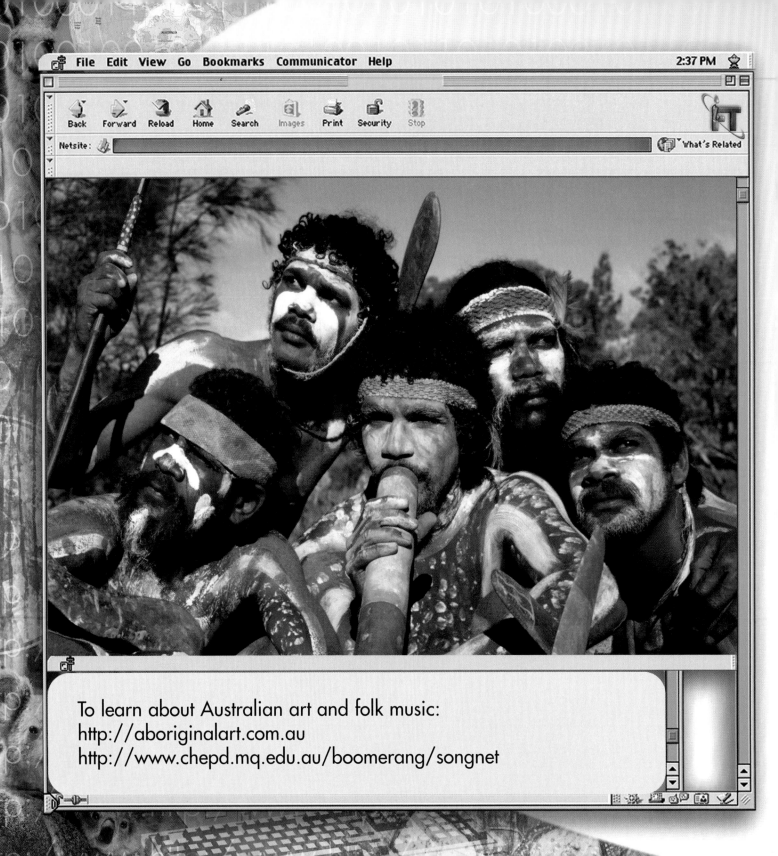

To learn about Australian art and folk music:
http://aboriginalart.com.au
http://www.chepd.mq.edu.au/boomerang/songnet

Rock Paintings
and Bush Ballads

Australia has a long, proud, artistic **tradition** that began with the aborigines. These native people are famous for their beautiful paintings on bark and rocks. They also play a long horn-like instrument called the didgeridoo. Have you ever read a bush ballad? A bush ballad is a long poem that describes the exciting adventures of life in the bush or in the deep Australian Outback in the late 1800s. Bush ballads are one type of Australian literature. Australians love to have fun, and it shows in their folk music. Australians are also well known for other kinds of literature, painting, architecture, and the films that they produce.

The aborigines in this photograph are nomads. One man is playing a musical instrument called the didgeridoo.

Back   Forward   Reload   Home   Search   Images   Print   Security   Stop

Netsite: What's Related

Keep Clicking!

You probably know a lot about Australia by now. The best part is that you've only just begun! Australia is changing every day. Australia is a beautiful country filled with neat animals, interesting people, and super-cool works of art. From aborigines to agriculture, from deserts to diamonds, from kangaroos to koalas, you can find it all in Australia! To stay on top of what's happening in "the land down under," visit Australian newspaper sites. Try The Australian On-Line at http://www.news.com.au. Or, click to Australia Online at http://australia-online.com. After all, you can never learn too much about Australia.

G L O S S A R Y

aborigines (ab-uh-RIJ-uh-neez) Original inhabitants of Australia.

architecture (AR-kih-tek-cher) The work of designing and constructing buildings.

coral reef (KOR-ul REEF) An underwater ridge of coral skeletons.

descent (dih-SENT) Being born into a certain family or ethnic group.

equator (ih-KWAY-tur) An imaginary line around Earth that separates it into two parts, North and South. The area around the equator is always hot.

ethnic group (ETH-nik GROOP) A group of people having the same race, culture, language, or belonging to the same country.

folk music (FOK MYU-zik) Music that is handed down among people.

geography (jee-AH-gruh-fee) The study of the features of Earth's surface, climate, continents, countries, and people.

hemisphere (HEM-uh-sfeer) One half of Earth.

industries (IN-des-treez) Businesses that make products or provide services.

landmass (LAND-mas) A very large area of land.

mineral (MIN-er-uhl) A natural ingredient from Earth's soil, such as coal or copper, that comes from the ground and is not a plant, animal, or other living thing.

nomads (NOH-madz) People who move from place to place with no single home.

plateau (plah-TOH) A broad, flat, high piece of land.

population (pop-yoo-LAY-shun) The number of people who live in a region.

tradition (truh-DIH-shun) A way of doing something that is passed down through the years.

23

Index

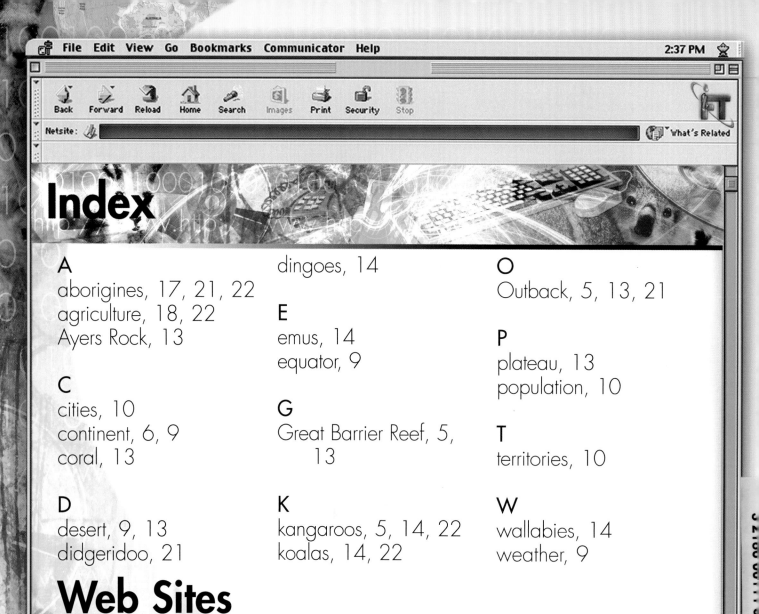

A
aborigines, 17, 21, 22
agriculture, 18, 22
Ayers Rock, 13

C
cities, 10
continent, 6, 9
coral, 13

D
desert, 9, 13
didgeridoo, 21

dingoes, 14

E
emus, 14
equator, 9

G
Great Barrier Reef, 5, 13

K
kangaroos, 5, 14, 22
koalas, 14, 22

O
Outback, 5, 13, 21

P
plateau, 13
population, 10

T
territories, 10

W
wallabies, 14
weather, 9

Web Sites

There are lots of exciting web sites about Australia. Check them out on the following pages: 7, 8, 11, 12, 15, 16, 19, 20, and 22.

24